YOU'LL FLIP, CHARLIE BROWN

YOU'LL FLIP, CHARLIE BROWN

A NEW *PEANUTS* BOOK

by Charles M. Schulz

HOLT, RINEHART AND WINSTON
New York • Chicago • San Francisco

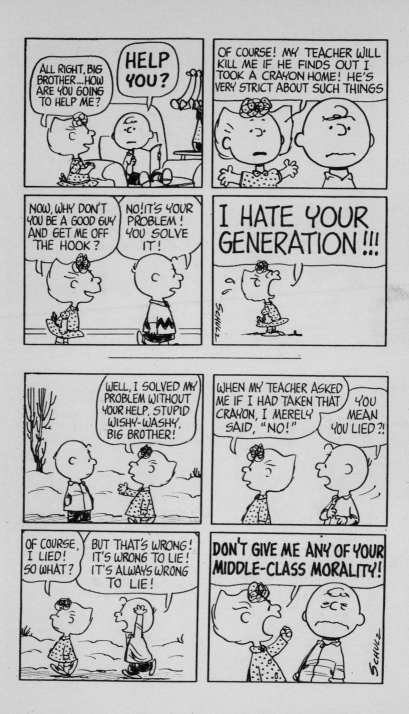

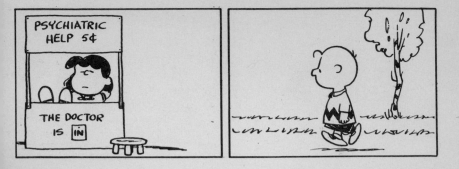

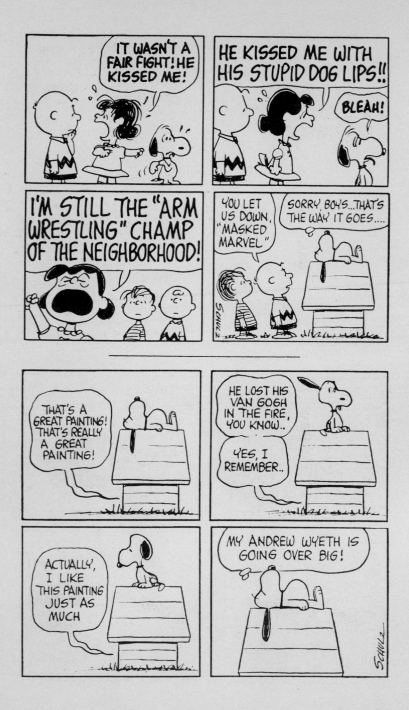

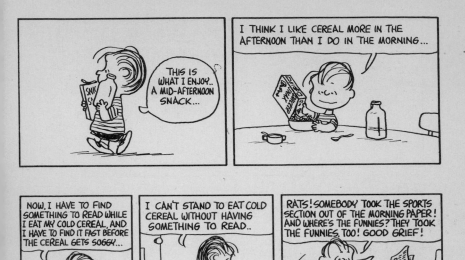

ARE YOU GOING TO BE A NEWSPAPER BOY WHEN YOU GET OLDER, CHARLIE BROWN?

WELL, I'D LIKE TO BE... YES, I THINK I'D LIKE TO HAVE MY OWN ROUTE..

THEN YOU SHOULD LEARN HOW TO ROLL AND FOLD A PAPER SO YOU CAN TOSS IT ONTO A DOOR STEP...HERE, LET ME SHOW YOU...

SEE, YOU FOLD IT ACROSS THE SECOND COLUMN LIKE THIS...THEN YOU ROLL IT LIKE THIS UNTIL YOU GET IT LIKE THIS, AND THEN YOU TUCK THIS PART IN HERE, AND TWIST IT LIKE THIS...

NOW YOU'RE ALL SET TO...

THROW IT!

ANOTHER THING YOU HAVE TO BE ABLE TO DO IS GET CUSTOMERS.. IF YOU WANT TO KNOW ABOUT THAT, FEEL FREE TO ASK..

THANK YOU..

SCHULZ

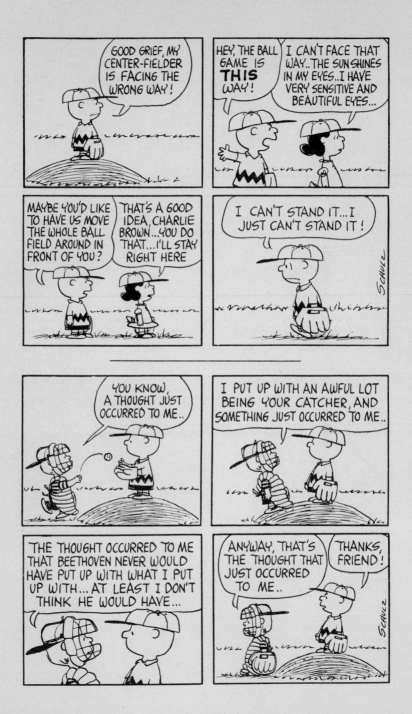

YOU'VE BEEN USING MY TOOTHBRUSH!

OH, DON'T BE SILLY! IT'S AN ELECTRIC TOOTHBRUSH, ISN'T IT? WELL, I JUST USED THE HANDLE!

SEE? THE TOOTHBRUSHES ARE INTERCHANGEABLE! WE JUST USE THE SAME HANDLE...

GOOD GRIEF!

BUT WHAT ABOUT THE ELECTRICITY? DO YOU EXPECT ME TO BRUSH MY TEETH WITH THE SAME DIRTY ELECTRICITY?!

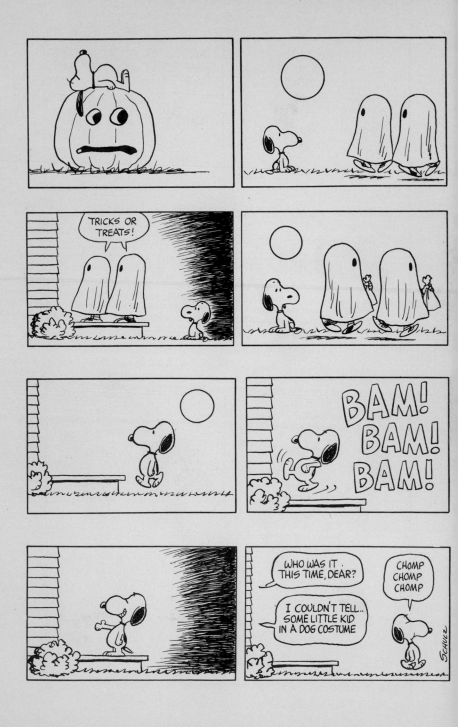

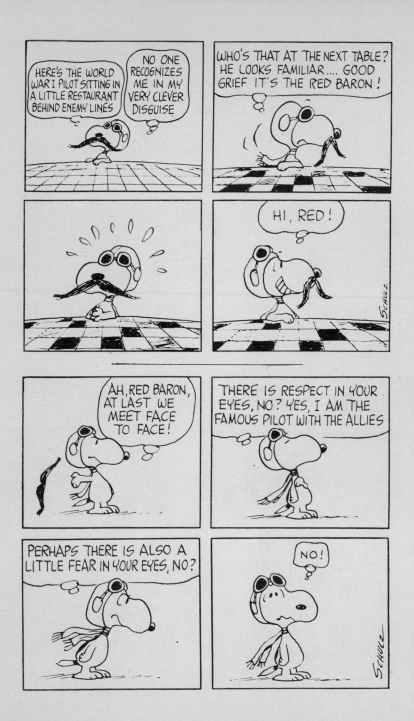

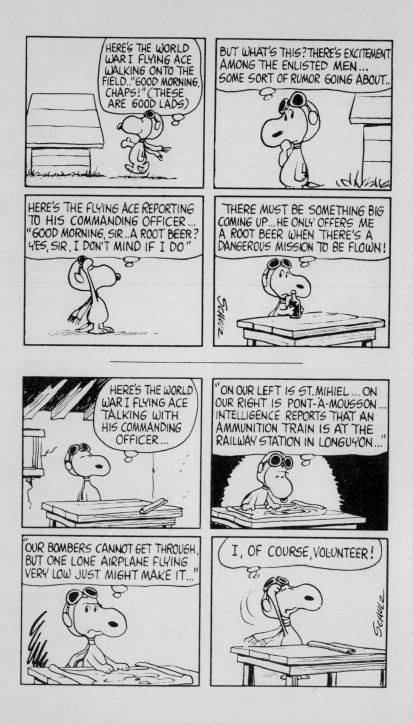

THEY'RE RIGHT... IT **IS** A LONG WAY TO TIPPERARY!

SCHULZ